Lyrics to the music outside

"The miserable have no other medicine
But only hope:
I've hope to live, and am prepared to die."

—William Shakespeare, *Measure for Measure*

"Humans carry around legacy behaviors and biases, jerry-rigged
holdovers from earlier stages of evolution that follow their own
obsolete rules. What seem like erratic, irrational choices are, in
fact, strategies created long ago for solving other kinds of problems.
We're all trapped in the bodies of sly, social-climbing opportunists
shaped to survive the savanna by policing each other."

—Richard Powers, *The Overstory*

.

" When they kick at your front door
how you gonna come?
With your hands on your head
or on the trigger of your gun?"

—Paul Simonon (The Clash), 'The Guns of Brixton'

considering sixty

years I looked out a flagstone
to use as a roof for the hibernaculum
I was creating for any amphibians
who might happen to make a home
in the garden now there is a pond
to satisfy their want of living water

thought of all the changes that occurred
over your lifetime, though nothing so drastic
as beginning with a life aquatic
has happened to you two—

or has it?   —for everything
changes so fast in the days we inhabit
that what we want becomes the familiar
and need is of the one who is always there

and as I dug out a hollow, and lined it
with new mown grass, soft, and damp, and some dry
raspberry stalks I had cut, and kept, over winter
without knowing why, an answer

stole into mind in the way that life will
                                        —given time
occupy a space, and make it breathe flowers
from the air, warmth from the earth, memories
from all that has happened
                                        —and you telling
almost the last time we were together
that you have been lucky in life
finding each other, and making such a
good place
                    —that 60 years is not enough
how could it be?
when there is love
and though it is unwise to meet face to face
in these times of pandemic
it was as though you were both standing there with me

you always will be

a wasps nest

when I saw that the wasp nest has
broken or the greater part of it has
come away on the last day of September
lays out on the short satisfying grass

the thin membrane of cells unerringly
exposed as a matrix of busy mothering become
empty houses the occupants having flown
the fluent air from windows that stare
blank-eyed such a drone architecture
as grey lights the growing dark—

this dancing mind jives on the wooden box
we used to keep all those papers in
that slept like water in a glass can . . .
the children's birth certificates, and so on . . .

it must have run afloat on the rapids
under-stairs or drowned in a cupboard..
the lost . . . honey coloured . . .
box your father made
of box wood   plain and glazed

it had always floated to the surface
when we first moved in
was now buried somewhere under the years
of nothing more than living

and you stand before me saying
that all the letters you most wanted to keep
the ones that would sting your eyes
                              were put to sleep
inside of it   without reply . . .

lockdown bird.

this dun

brown speckled feather flower has
a black-bead eye
                          a polka-dot eye-
popping blinking appetite
                                    for the ripened dark sweet
jostaberries, gulping all
                          about it,
                                    the dancing juvenile
silently regards us outsiders,
                          appears unconcerned
                                              unfrit
                                              at how close we are

flights balled breath tremble stares at the sweet
plump stars tagged to limbs all about it
not shielding nor hiding
                                    infant to the world

a seed spreader in harness
                          busily occupied
                                              with filling at source,
like the idea
                    inflated of itself being all ruffled
                                                        curiosity
at a wealth weighs on every
swaying branch,
                          it disappears to reappear,
                                    disappear, reappear
exhausts every traunch
                          of this its own-made territory
of the here and now,
                          no beggar, nor a thief

                                    escaping anyhow

this tree had flat shoes

'flatees' she would call them
broad not thin that tapered in
to the unbroken moss and liverwort covered earth
where crawling things make
something of themselves
apparently out of nothing

just like

she had all of that thicken and rise
foliage and flowers   some-time
snatched from the air like a promise

as if thought could be solid drinking light

she would swallow streams making them
flow up her throat canals in defiance
of gravity itself

transported by affinity alone

until as easy on the ear exhalations of joy they became
cloud-form
laden with chemical speech saying
all of those things one life might say to another

she moves tenderly seeking a way between obstructions
joining strut limb to limb   long toe to toe

knowing
something of the frisson of the little movements

inside her sleeve
outside her arms reach

she was always one for sensible shoes
                                   small steps
                                        gentle exercises
stretching out slowly as far as she could go and then coming

         to rest
by the smallest of increments   orienting
herself to the sun and easing through   outside of notice

where green and sappy thought lives
as the movement of air through leaves
its vellum moss folds of consideration
lichen flecked caught in the act of vanishing

the weight

of the various orders and combinations of words
found and chosen to keep, broke
three wooden shelves, splitting one
of the shelves of the bookcase assembled
one day from a kit bought on the net

the wood was thin
the pre-drilled holes and pins were not exactly a match

yet it had seemed sufficient
to hold contained all of that whose only purpose is
when all is said and done
to break free, and live again

there are streams are stars bound
ceaselessly changed and endlessly changing

six steel brackets, a hammer, twelve screws, and a screwdriver are
all it takes to cage them in

out of focus

the wholly manual
bicycle
standing outside of this double glazed window
and down two storeys
chains

it is propped on its short metal leg, and bent foot
attached by a thick steel
cable lock to a metal tube that slots
into the concrete
pavement at both ends after
circling up over itself to beg mid-air
in a line becoming a wave

the handlebars are like those Picasso
used to make the bulls horns
of a sculpture he once saw at the Picasso
museum in Paris

the cream coloured tyres are fully inflated
and although there is no bell no ting
it weighs
as it stands and stares fully serviced and tweeked
the wheels realigned, brakes sorted, seat adjusted
everything balanced

it is now faster
than it was
and is waiting on events that
have
or have not
to come to pass

although going so fast can only mean that he will see less
he will use it

in this light

night-fishing is
      unpredictable

tides turn
      a skin of dew
return
      the shy moon

to the delta of her wrist
the tributaries of her fingers

and her ankles
      her ankles that owe nothing—

what touches
      loosening ribs cage
takes breath

in waves
      of flame
as things are breaking down

out—somewhere—beyond
the hem of sober contemplation

open

thoughts dappled green
encroachments of over—
leaving shade

                                     fall

to where flowing dark
deeps cool and curl

slowly carry
water boatmen scurrying
beat paddle legs, diving
beetles, and all
tarried manner of beings
meandering in ways
they circle about

whatever hard is
encountered will score
cares in—

the fallen white
stippled petal on the ground is
sodden with a rain
still falls
as the sky brightens
                              momentarily
grey cloud drifting aside
reveals the white of an open sky

what passion eats away
so quickly that by the next day all is gone

the white that was a kind of cream
almost velvet fragile-ridged skin
                                             breaking apart
outside of focus
somehow reached in and struck a claim
at the heart

and while diminishing startled a flame
as if even sodden with rain it was a kind of kindling
could not be smudged out

Cafe song.

for Graham who likes a rhyme

The baby in the high-chair chews a fist
shakes arms and legs, eats veggie crisps

looks from blue-eyes to other eyes
looses a voice that neither laughs nor cries

beyond the window in the rain a chugger waves
at passers by passing as they might a grave

seeing me at the window, she smiles, and waves
I smile back, no-one is saved

a poster on the wall shouts that 'things fall apart'
a man sits safe and dry with a bird for a heart

trying out the steady measure of his bones
on a screen a survivor tries to make a home

while the collective mind of a forest burns
there is no harm in us, no harm in us, no harm

the plot
('and players')

is having an unusual year, though what's usual these days
of torrential rain following record breaking hot

it has one after another strange failure—Beetroot
promising much set sail only to remain in dock

too small to clot soil to the gob stopper dark
of a bloody-purple heart   Spinach roasted on a bed

of parched earth, then drowned
in a wet rots roots and leaves

                all bolt to seed, along with chard
                      and lettuce . . .

nothing satisfies
whatever balance there was is lost

all ideas of good surplus fly
                with the imaginary bees

while change changes outside of knowing, so swiftly
it must be that the usual method of doing's finished

for the weather we turned capricious has lit the stage
and it's throwing or its torrents or its burning rage

catalogue for the illusory future.

at the far end, though there is no far end, is Comfrey
wind seeded burst-blends of green transplanted from wherever
to a military line, in some places a double line, of thick
high growing bristle haired stems and coarse leafs and blue
and purple bee-sucked head drop flowers separating this
allotted space, and the next

at the far corner of the far end a redcurrant muscled
sidling out spreading about an apple a white currant and some
raspberries the last of those that tunnelled under fired up in cane-
breaking lofty entanglements through lapping branches to poke
out tousled heads and make delicate-blown cusp-projections
                                                    of future white

at the far end, before the Comfrey, is a cleared space light
concentrates potatoes shallow-buried
where sanguine ants and black beetles patrol as a robin rests
on the low leaf-swirl of an apple branch, and will come
mote if hurry of thrum-worn goldcrest dunnock blackbird thrush

at the far end strawberries take on buttercup dandelion
oregano marjoram chive mint herb-robert nettle bindweed
and dock running quick threads, wicks a greening hurl of earth

at the far end dolls-hairbrush-voles dart cover to cover
and snails slither or snug under flap-leaf like jewelled stones
the soft leather underbellies retracting silently while a relish
of absurdly innovative assemblies of insects sound about hot

at the far end a plastic container half-cut
of a two-litre bottle fills with water greens with moss

at the far end viridescent lichen patches like dry stone the stems
and branches of a past flowering white currant whose
profusion overflows streams down droplets on finely nodal stems

at the far end stones rocks and half bricks are rubble left
to brambleoaksorrelwaspcrowmothhazelpupawormpoppiepoppiepoppie
from unknown constructions overlooked or dumped
onto mud that is worms is grubs is beetles is flesh and bone

at the far end skeletal spiders tender fire webs, the fuse-
threads feeding quietly communicatively stringing disparate things
even us

this is a place with no maps
nothing is exiled vacant unrelated or can be contained

close by the far end just beyond the bullfinch rest
are caterpillars milked by ants and in a certain place
readies a pregnant puffball swelled to a pale white round
balloon taller than a pencil
as big as a football—full

sex amongst the grasses and birdsfoot trefoil
of a common path

untethered it is
the smooth clean intimate styrofoam head of a man blind
of feature dry of flesh dry of skin naked closed and dumb
who thinks itself enough raised up weakly sprung
of the black earth, waiting to be lifted
to feel the weight of itself, the pain of rising, the heat
of an unhoming

at the far end that is not rooted
                                        light
                                                en
                                                        er
                                                                gies
of a sun locked in seeds and spores ride the air

soon at the far end—over the edge
seas of rain troubling will wash the rich loam to a melt a foam
of the known and unknown
world concentrated to a bloom on tides that scour flat
an emptiness where
fasted winds feast on what scraps remain
under the volatile smouldering eye of a sun—
as innocent injured earth—clown residency over—empties

                                        life's sustaining clamour
                            of vital call and answer
                silenced

Opium Poppies

ran wild through the allotment.
Heads facing all together on mild green
stalks trembled in the breeze at the far end
of spring. The delicate mauve

skirts, a hurry of four petals, will
drop on being roughed at all, by hand
or wind, leaving chased flower-heads
to swell from a crib to a rattling globe
that tops frail-haired slender stems—
all tightly wound upended pendulums.

Unlooked for they are flags of resistance.
The wild returning. Each a little chaos—
of nothing is meaningless, and yes
they fill up Mole days, like hope does.

happen upon a frog

big as a closed fist, or beating heart
the lung-skin having within it every hue of green
the still of it waiting
composed, seeming to know it is seen

no doubt there are others hidden amidst the reaching
knots that tangle
to the unprotected light
watching from under buttercup, nettle, and marjoram
quickening

considering shadows change
it bobs
                                                              and
with easy flex stretching lengthening legs into propulsion
                                                    disappears—

everything else remains,
 and blood
blood kicks in the veins

bats.

overwinter the plums, all ignored
shrank to bat like husks
sleeping fixed to the branches
in the scraped light

dried out
they clacked dryly against each other
the wind tugging their umbilicals

disappeared wreathed in white early flowers
were found hiding in the profusion when
trees were reborn

these corpses of sweet ones
overlooked late summer's swells are
changed utterly now

with skins
all of white spores and pin-head orange
eggs waiting

they are become both beginning and end
birth and death

Gooseberry roots, as thick as a closed fist

ran on, under, and on . . .

Cut back the bushes are raw knuckles rising from
the bared earth, and each arm
clothed in silence, is a lost thing hiding
in plain view. There is no disguising
how ugly they are. Each stump
the hooked offspring of a hacksaw
raises one claw after another . . .

Dug out and pity mixes with the blood
running from the wounds the thorns made.

As an offering the hole is filled with part decayed
Comfrey, and is then made good.

Northern words are like this, deep-rooted, barbed, dangerous,
without warning they can rip in leaving a hurt under the skin.

the newt

was made of the pond in a way it was
mud of the bottom come
up to the surface
risen from dark folds to consider us
slender, less than half a thumb
a contained vastness

or dark sliver of limber tongue cut out of a throat
now inhabited by others

something of the distant unreliable past stares
to see if anything of matter remains
intact and usable
how everything has become mixed up
freed from the demands of unity or any idea
                                        of place

a flood filled and wet the banked up
dust to a clot-weld of what was

a realm of nothing firm
nothing at all that is not contingent, or continuous

play

a mouse out of an unfilled place
in the high stone wall where the path runs

by the river,   the river
clear as light   plays

over rounded stones   closed purses
of the deeps where

reflections strut and turn awry

a white willow high in a gossip of crowded heads
nettle make   pushes
green from a broken bough
whose threads freed needle the air
to trail the wind in streaming repair

another mouse, perhaps a clutch, will be
immured somewhere else, close by

conjunctions of fierce wild affinity
                          Joy   Joy   Joy

a part of a diaspora

fronds of fern sprouting from the stone wall
on long lane
fill the crannies and gaps in
what has become decayed

even the weighty stones of the wall migrated
                                                    years ago
having abandoned what was a skirmishing border of sorts
separating an empire from its 'barbarian' others

seasons of cracking ice and blistering sun
awaken in this fern like long attritions

thought stirs to earthen grit
the firing substrate—what

seeds and dry matter's are set inside of it

--

--

a rabbit pattered field started it
running—that and what remains
of a bonfire in one corner, the
charred wood and soot
blackened stones make the place
one of withdrawal, and regret
like the moors and the quarry
before the firing range, its red
flags flying warning on firing days
stopping the hunt for spent cartridges
when trespass was a way of life
and the only notion of private was
bound up in the words them and us

--

the

trees

naked barbed shards were all that remained of what had been
a forest
covering the earth in a shelter of shade that used to blink open
to flower
in a growth that happened to capture sunlight and rain

they were memory
in the way that water, water falling, and the movement of water
is memory—is a holding to what has been that is always
changed, changing in the way that the part ivy—
strangle struggled free straggle of branches that was high
above a beetle crawling outbreak of bluebell, and others—was a library

I remember moving in
between one tree and another light dimmed and winked down
through the puzzle insect hum of branches so that looking high
a halo sun would appear framed by leaves crossed by branches

twig dry rustling the crackle marked movement of each way impeded
is a reaching growth for light whose breath
scents the air so taste is furred with pollen and sharp sweet bark

in the dense crowd a vast communion cools everything in the reason
of silence, of constellations buds curling tight to contain
every hint of death—such erotic realisations of air

while outside irritations of crows fretted about the forest edges
and occupied the low meadows across cemetery roads

walking out

from the sky-to-floor enclosure of tree shade
the grass a vibrant green made
greener by rain's
soft fall, as if not wanting
to part with the air
or submit itself to gravities weighty law,
opened a door
to crow's caw, blackbirds throaty song, and more
that populate the air—

and this is where we are
where moss enlivens tree bark
where ivy clings to stem and makes
its root a foot again

waiting, not for the rain to pass—
what is that to us?

watching the beech leaves stilted dance
stringed up as they are until autumn

almost heart shaped—

most often holed by something unknown

Untitled 1

wounded thunder groaned behind a grey unsettling
impermanence, growled like clay under a rivers torque
and bent turned sound rebounded from the green
to sound again, assembling forces unseen beyond what was
a mountain, a place that none could cross
until tunnelling in the screw machines forced a way
for other machines that carry as they destroy
what distance was, and silence ends in a whine
continuous as they transport goods from wherever
labour is the cheapest, to where they claim the highest price

Untitled 2

in a frame of small clearances
at night
a pin point on the map
grass and trees perspire
loosing in a little heat
words appeared
before any thought of them

oleogenous gulls beyond the pier.

on the toll road where
land curves
to a serpents head
she walks beside the rock face to the snouts end
rounds the bend
disappears
seeking what is out of sight

gulls wheel and dive the heights
off-shore

in the distance white wind turbines turn
so many waving arms

sea wears a grey blue turquoise brown
implacable face that is
a surface, always changing

wind, taking
something no-one can hear
out over the sea
undercover of the distant drumming music of the pier
thins, the
rising cloud loosed
from the burdens of water vapour—
each burgeoning droplets singular desire
to cohere
prickles skin cold leaving a sheen—
a quickening lick of salt,
is a stealth visitor stealing

away with the goods—
minerals, elements, the fruits
of a scour through the porous earth where
copper mines dug out with child labour are
a reminder of us

the air is scented by onions

gathered bunches at the window, tied long
throated stems, each bulbous stopper arrested in
tumbling is a vacantly absorbing sheer white
emitting stillness at the centre, each has weight
and a mass that appears to affect the movement of the light
as if there is something bright at its core

they reek of vinegar, of time, the way that luminous
thick wax does when the lit wick is sunk deep
within the body of a much used candle

they have been lifted, carried here, washed carefully, and stripped
of a dry-papery skin

in the early morning they haunt the air acridly telling
how death, and the dead, share everything

casually, indifferently, all about us

Buenas noches

what is missing
in the internal dark

when the doors unlocked and open
are closed and locked again

when footsteps sounding on the concrete stair
are heard overhead   then under

as water airs from shower geysers

is the occasional lonely wakefulness
of the early morning bus

and greys congruent coalescence to light birds
singing birds first song—this

is what is missing—is what is missed

all of the ingredients

waited for kettles first boil as he put on his shoes
opened the door

bought in the spout-less green watering can and left it
babbling at the sink

made a green tea and putting a bagel on a plate
stepped outside into the faint

sun to water
whatever he thought fragile before she became

strong enough to burn

if

he'd known she would leave sour-dough bread
cooling safe inside

the upturned dome of a steel mixing bowl
beside white onions attached by thin ribbons

to a pin above the kitchen window
that she will look through   amused

as starlings work the lawn hopping sideways

then forward in the early morn

he would have stayed until the weather set
though the moons bare eye wet the sky

Neighbourhood.

seeing her was dangerous
he knew it

they lived their young years
streets apart

were suckled by the same
cacophonous din

the too many made
crammed in

to the one seam
that music beat out of

it crossed partition fences
entered their veins

a shared language
of lost names and no names

Two haiku that just happened and one that didn't.

for David Simmons

1

man sits in a tent
under a sun filled blue sky
embracing his faults

2

a tree in a field
transubstantiation is
raising an acorn

3

bring him an army
to take privilege and wealth
he will gift you peace

1987 Jon K Clark made a stained glass window

the mottled pale grey olive light brown kind of sky
                              'have you ever seen such a sky?'
is opaque, like glass used to be at the bottom of old bottles
back when all bottles were individually blown
by craftsmen
                    it has twenty one

speckled blue bodied fish swimming left to right

they have bluntly armoured heads and thick
yellow lips, yellow fins, flecked sides
                                        quick staring eyes

'or at least the eye of every fish you see is quick,
                                              and stares'

having leapt they are
moving through a light that floods to illuminate

these oblates that have broken apart
                    from the deep blue
                                        that birthed
and always sustained
                    pulled by migrations urge

they muster needing little
                    a counsel of one will
                              as primitive and tender
                                        as a promise

over the river.

herons long legs swallowed are
of the deep
having waded in where water joins water

shakes ruffle down
and as he raises the periscope of his neck
his arrow head swivels attending

what is all around in a state of rest
until that stiff stuffiness returns
that is a lure

standing all shoulders like one delivering a writ
who stays on having knocked three times at the door

he waits in a calculated way that requires little
is confident that there must come an answer

that even now, at the end of day, there will be more

Untitled 3

we follow the dry earth
path to where a tangled strength of
tree root holds the flaky soil
about the rabbit holes the children
peer in for signs of occupation

light came
after travelling its vast distances
out of the trees on the downs
where Libby runs and Johnny catches
hugs, and they jump into shapes
and the blue green
lichen clustered on the branches above us
catches fire

the way through the vineyard is bolted
the closely cropped vines standing guard in measured lines

off the wall.

a man who would stand looking
out at the waters edge
the waves lapping at his feet
a weatherman discreetly out

has breakfasted on trumpets, toast and marmalade
orange juice, green tea, and some
of the strawberries she bought a large tray of
to be eaten quick, before they go off

small birds, finches of some sort, shelter
like fat flutes, with the wasps, under the bearded
canopy outside
as the rain drips in thin streams to the ground

without coats or umbrellas there is a hurrying blur
                                        to shops, and cafes
a waiting looking out from doorways

while the street itself, become slick and shiny
swishes wet winded waves
                            of cars and buses by

in a light charged, that is sullied as the rain

turning everyday pavements from dust to shine

allowing reflections that leap out into nothing

bramble growing

releases energies of the stone
as if plugging directly into the mains
fusing and spiking out

is a green matter exuded and running all about
                                        in separating veins
that tremble in sunlight like shadow
seeking and rooting by fretful touch

            it twists a bind round what proves sufficient
and barbed it hooks without eyes
                                    unerringly
                                            tears and rips

whatever cannot be worked through is worked over—
chthonic stone satisfies

                    wrought iron fence posts
                        rubbish and struts interred or half buried
anchor the spool to out its gifted sp
                            lin
                            te
                            ry
                                threads

riddling its own intransigent purposes
having carried itself within itself it lies
                                    idle
                            or climbs
knowing every touch every handshake
                            will extract a penalty
each clot of blood
                    a wary child

wounds like explosive thought troubled into snagging limbs
                                              will flay

unintelligibly it bounds and gantries idiosyncratically through
                    the grass chasing
                              the light making
                                        dark fruit

that glistens like black glass
                    clustered bomblets curious
                              to bloody the mouth

engorged black moons dropping like hearts
are a tacky black language that seeds and surges

sweet through the unmapped place

          as hope does, perhaps

teasing out what is unaltered, unalterable, what lasts

is the mistle thrush so named because
it consumes mistletoe berries and shits
the seeds out onto the branches
of the particular tree that mistletoe needs
to propagate the next generation?

there is one

flies from the trees that flank the lane
and follows the curve of the hill we climb
to descend again before climbing st ann's

it seems appropriate the way of things are
that the seeds should pass through the arse
before the life they contain can spring

even that they feed parasitically seems
to be relevant—

to bear

relation to how we are, and whatever
virus it is that we carry inside of us

Ivy

Hard days striking pyramid flowers from the way
breaking towering green stalks poked vainly past leafy stems
uprooting a strangling morass that cut back reveals
colonies of snails clustered tight, hid safe, and spiders
scurrying from branch to brick tenderly skeletal
their webs fluttering flags of grey that catch the bright sunlight
of a dying summers day—light falling only to rise again
warmed and mocking those holding to a hardened past
fastened by the millipede tendrils that line the cracked patina
of old wall to run, hanging, in the air, brushing hands
with a fine dust of age so rich it clogs the lungs and slows the veins
to an old pulse that begs a change, a change

swollen blood berries sign another growth each clot shiny
and exposed, its stems hooked sharp with hungry thorns to
graze and pierce, protecting them from soft skin

loose bricks fixed in place after a stand of a hundred years
are bones to an invader that climbed, covered, crumbled,
and clothed them in green and black, brought in other refugees
from the blocked light, and then cascaded to ground
to force victory with a stamp of its twisted, gnarled, foot

now a cautious shuffler unused to its ploughed furrow feels
with chisel and saw to prise and pull apart, peeling stems to cut
so that keener feet can rise in place of the long dead and reverse
a deathly tread—an early release of blood saps strength
with clouded thoughts of work and bed, but the ivy holds
while others with a mornin' smile or nod pass by on the pavement's
tacky rings of autumn that drop from high leaves like shadows

to hold them for an instant from the light, aware of broken apples
bruised brown that invite younger feet, or bright suddenly call butterflies
to erratic flight against the stiff breeze starting branches to motion
whipping up the leaves, directing eyes to chase winged eyes
past the bird lovers who gather on this day each month, religiously,
flocking to share caged passions, their feathered triumphs
carried before them in the last of the good light

lost to this in a pollen haze of work, while each detail points
and plays in the sun that catches easy strollers
rolling slowly through their days, the cutting carries on

Heron

6th

Saw a heron eat a little slither
    of the silver river

9th

Maybe the heron that I thought a man
    is, was a woman
    —somehow melancholy
when cloud obscures the sun it is
curiously a shroud raised upright on the water
and when the light is full on
the unlikely brand of itself appears
root legs cutting against all baffled direction
planted bloodless feet toes holding
to the silt river bed. Is it
a woman weeping?

I see her sometimes standing—alone
a shabby kind of a creature—not
wandering—not old—not young

thorny, so that to reach out and touch her
she will snap—beyond speech—
her sharp beak at the Gulls
concerted diving
inorder to drive her from this thin spit
she has claimed hers, more an island really
      —not even a dot on a map
      as the earth is lost on a star map

a raised up held fast loose rest of shingles
concentrated, fixed to a place by the roots
of some low scrub
so that when the river is low even the cows come
down here to nibble at some nameless herb

           they can find no-where else.

Mayflies

A bridge of orange clay
on a steel tubular frame
is where mayflies flit.

Delicate sets of wings
beat asynchronously
about each planet's

long tapering body
—a fidget of the air,
eccentric and giddy,

moving above the water
it hatched out of.
Polished steel and dull clay

worked into position
joins beginning to end,
has a purpose in a

way the slow running
river, and dithering
Mayflies do not.

The river eats
into the rough banks
that peel away

on either side,
gorges itself each high tide.
Mayflies sip at

dead shivers of air,
devils hanging there
learning its language

Wasp.

A faint buzzing at the ears
uncomfortably nears

It is a mystery how they keep on coming in

I would throw them out
all of them
astonished pieces
of a larger thing

What a society is
is something that coheres

These yellow and black bands are a mark, perhaps
of self sacrificing

The feared sting being something
that must be taken on

drawn out of them
from the rapture of the bodies spindle

its drill precision
urgently braced within the legs rigging

There is no knowing the thing apart
unmassed, outside of its cauldron

One, undone,
has broken the muttered vow of its own

making to surrender all thought of motion
and be paper-dry and brittle

A sculpture on the ledge
its worrying head black metal

conjuring tree-bug

the man seated amongst trees

hair and beard straggled with leaves
green hat flecked with blues and greys
optimistic sap of pocket days
like myrrh waits for what will be to be
for the machines to come that topple trees
to clear a way for roads or farms
or factories by doing harm

sees the ants climb boughs that feed
the birds who roost eating seed

a good order in the tangled branch and leaf
their grounded rooted reasoned grief

as toppling the anchors of the sky—we stop
life's wounded breath and all destroy

in the ordinarily intoxicated light

her head lights against his shoulder
lightening events in the spa town
where people take the waters
and brass bands play suffused melancholies
of blue green pools and the men
playing speed chess stop to watch

a girl pass
and listen as
little disturbances splash the pieces

in the bars they drink small beers
and cognac waiting for six o'clock

only to meet unexpectedly in the park
where it is too suffocating to whisper

down long streets of stone steps
where farmers bearing gifts of brandy reflect
on spies and absentmindedness

there are the dreamed confidences of touch
in darkened rooms rich with colour

the blue river making a sadness of five swans

curious devices.

these are the days of spiders webs

assertive pearled threads connecting
                              branch to hedge
wall to door frame

              seeing them
                     she says

'they will seek a mate
                  in the warm inside
discreetly set old lace
                  to catch dust in the high corners

look—there is beauty beckons
in the cold curiosity of the clustered jewels
                                      of their eyes'

long thin-legged crepuscular ones cantor rustling
                              out into the open
                                          creakily
run the edges of the sitting room
                              scuttle away

                  she names some—

though all are deaf to us
                  concerned only
                          with tending the nets of loneliness
they inhabit
          or retiring alert to self-imposed isolation

they rest limbs stretched across
the stringed instrument

                              of their own construction

which they do not play, preferring
to feed on other player's vibrations

always the optimists they follow
                the simple precept
                            make it and they will come

one was close, that is

laid out like a corpse the head touching
one wall, as toes
touched the one facing, and a wrapping sheet
under the feet to be warm
when night walls became porous and windspeech
happened, and owls hunted
mice or whatever in the wild beyond the wire

everything owned was kept at arm's distance
was reached for to touch and know
was familiar of the day that there might be escape

the road was an ear and people
walked by and talked
to each other beyond the black
iron of the fire
place saying things they
could listen to
as they lay waiting for sleep

or lazily

letting the day roll past and on
in the way they could then when there was
so-much to do just to stretch
what they had to make what was needed

when trees were banished to the park
of weekends, or to the ends
of train journeys cut
from where nothing was fingers
combing the air

shaping thought that it might live there
quiet   outside of reason

Coconut

1.

A bit like coconut matting, remember, from PE
In primary school, that's what the surface looked like
Brown, almost the same colour, but a little darker
Probably because it's wet, that's why I thought it
Dead, a dead thing, was alive and now it's just a skin
Full of methane from all that grass they eat
Four stomachs make it float that way, head under
Legs trailed, body a barrel, moving quite fast too
Down the centre of the river faster than you'd think
Think it was a young one, a calf maybe, a heifer
Taken by the water, it could have been part of a tree
Except it was not that shape, and seemed to have hair
A bit like coconut matting, remember, from PE

2.

sky is sky and that kind of cloud that mists away to nothing.
near sound is the cries of children playing and far is traffic noise, a steer.
wind winds through the trees softly moaning as if accustomed
to this place and its tasks of carrying, as if pleased
to be by the river on this day when such a weight of water is shifting
slowly, inexorably, atom by atom, whole matrices of them, see
himalayan balsam bows pink headedly and cow parsley stiffly resists
refusing all but the slightest nod of its white ennobled head.
there is a soapy scum on the surface
of the water just here, it drifts,
passes two lovers on a bench who are having one of those conversations
that bring two heads so close together that their foreheads touch
and the sides of their bodies touch and they clasp hands.
across is a heron
standing alone as still as stone, or rather as a fine bone
sculpture sited and unmoving—its dull reflection
has no detail but colours the surface, and also is still in the passing.
there is a black flash
above the one of its eyes that face this way, another
black flash above the hunched in wing, all else
is white but for the grey of the wing and the pink legs that are rods
wavering and disappearing.

I wait. it waits. we are waiting

3.

how to address the heavy cattle
curious slap-bellied hulks

who patiently feed on pasture
without the remedy of herb and weed

waiting for the fraught pull of milk coming
in that will carry them on

to the concrete sucking shed
along the usual

truculent rough cobbled lane where the barking dog warns
every stranger savouring the sweet ordure the air

who strays here
to be aware of the ways in and out

across the cobbles water articulates
dirty streams where shitty streaked green-brown run-offs

slough fizzing with flies

whoever closes the gate sliding the bolt all of the way home
                                        leaving
the low breathy slung-bellied who are
legs to fetlock awkward

who sees sorrow gather
in the gutters and banked up skies of their staring eyes

the sorely-used dugs hot for calves only bred for slaughter

is utterly changed

Day

television woman tells iran
has seized one of our oil tankers
off the strait of hormuz

blueberries out the back wait
as the sun ripens
to make green blue

K reads Rachel Carson's silent spring
pausing to take small doses in
while a female blackbird with a cocked head

witnesses an uprising of sprongs of hedge
sees a snail retract inside its cave

the profusion in this small space
over-spills borders that reach

rooks sidle in to drink the gutter
water of the house opposite   What are we doing

knowing the harm—

Untitled 4

bristle touched thing of night not missed o-sun of
this darked side every warm thing is shouldering close soft burls
flaptendernesses brush past all constants and amass just behind
out o-reach breathe streams and in the dum-dum-dum stringings
of voice o-stretched as ambulatory crashingscapes of falling
trees out vine pull weeds leafclothed while passing a season
on seasons in graphical-precision is stoked dust-rearing
childnesses so stripingly barren and absented that there is no
sense of any having been any having o-all is buried o-
is unborned is was and is not

Whenever

Wednesday would clean
the varnished body
of the dark piano
under the lean
African statuettes
who had settled there

to stand
blind eyed and silent

a collapsible music stand
moved aside
to occupy the already
pregnant air

listened to the treble
voices of the street,

noticed that on top
of the pile of sheet—

music is a Jamaican
folk song—Mango Feet

what was outside

snuck in
curious of the warm
when she got up
showered, made up
and prepared
for work's narrow grief

waited
a poor fit
occupying her space
as she rushed out
calling

explored
the hollow caves
she had been
soaking
in the heat

the waves
lapping his feet
tickled the stones
on the beach
until there was a fossil
inside each

'anapha'

amongst the unclean
        they taste fishy.

Apparently
are what you'd expect of such 'stumpy clothed walking sticks.'
Wading sticks more like making me think of stilt houses.
        Chinese paintings,
           or their bright silk-embroidered blouses.

It seems too much of a projection
        out from the hunched
           shoulders, and on
       —to gloom, or even—dejection
when necessarily they are most often lone

        waiting snipers!

Bird clued to fire off a strike
        is long in habit.
           Strides patient looking.
Is delicately poised
        to sunder the scrubby surface and shallow weeds
           now.

Still hungering
        takes to flight,
           and is soon high and lost to sight.

All the days
        it looks
           to feed.

Untitled 5

anonymous grass sways as stillness winds place to place

1st December . . .

white infiltrates the unprotected air

unhomed the birds sink into footprints
                    declining to sing

horses that shivered in thin
            life preservers, have left us

every thing is replaced by its familiar
                    a bulked up white replica
in an emulsion of dips and scuds
turned by the light
            to a strange glaze
                    that crackles on rooftops
                            skids and falls
                                    as if greased
                                            from laden branches
                            and is replaced

the deadened ground dirties
                    tamped underfoot
            by those who ghost amongst the close
                            clustering trees
every rushing sound
                    wakes an echo
lethargic ideas of thinness
                    brittleness
            sinking through the levels
                    drains
as the filtering days and nights
                    tremble

Peace Lily

if she should moan
softly for the lack of water
                              I would start
to water her

whose leaves hang like rags
fretting and fiddling
as if they were thoughts

transplanted
the roots have coiled and thickened
about themselves, and spread

to the soil from under the old wall
where the soft bricks are breaking
and the clay and limestone mortar split
into its constituents, is leached
in tiny amounts night and day

every unheard cry is a failure
of the water stopped behind the tap

the little one

was a hand to hold
waiting all together at the stop

for the bus that would take them up
the hill to the turning point

where the driver would wait to change
and where they disembarked to cross the space
and pass the graves
in the blackness of the spreading trees

to the ambiguous rivers crossing place
where they parted ways, always

Untitled 6

for George

as a boy he'd developed a theory
that brains grow in the way trees do
by taking something of each day
that is layered on top of all the others
to make a shell that hardens over time

he had seen the black walnut trees
in Spain that are farmed for cork
and liked that each day was an outer crust
becoming more and more difficult to drill
through back to the distant past

that the outer crust was a forming present
of unstable plates still   and moving
that would colour and distort like water
or a lens affecting every gaze within

he was unconvinced by the spaghetti junction
of neural pathways and synaptic connections
that thought comprised of nerve impulses
and chemical releases   liking instead

to picture thoughts pressed out of cork
as bottle stoppers   hold in
those other thoughts that might occur
that rise up then as an explosion of corks

flying like birds from the branches of a tree

Jasmine

when the country where she was born failed
and had to be bailed out

her legs failed her in the night
she was discovered on the floor

cold and crying
in so confused a state

it took a while for her to be calm, and forget
the helplessness that overcame

to be clean again, and warm
eat and drink

that the feeble strength might return
to endure the long dark

and wait for the change to come
that rides the air with jasmine blossom

'class'

was something that you might be taught
to aspire to, once, they used to say
'she's got class, that lass,' appreciatively
but yesterday saw them laughing
all the millionaires that govern us
as they took away half a million jobs
cut the benefits of those with none
laughed and fucked off to their stately homes

Untitled 7

everything darkens under a rain
as promiscuous as shot glasses ricocheting
off all of the surfaces, and there is slowed lead
impacting dully, the thud
of it so hard that it both drenches
                                        and bounces
instantaneously changing
                    and wipes
                            all the slates clean
recoils in sympathetic flows
                    that fill the gutters and the drains
and attends to all those small things outstanding
for too long
            the cracked parapets,
                            broken teeth
                                        missing slates
and all of the gaps in the cement,
                            revelling in the brittleness
picked at and probed as if to wash
away the fabric of the house,
                        its upstart architecture,
bones, and all
            those soft trappings hid safely within
                        away then
                            from unsure foundations

In the night

somewhere on the right
between spine and ribbings
air is kettled.

It has been four days—
a sharp pain resides
without relief, except

every now and then an agent-
provocateur escapes the enduring lines
of resistance to rejoin

and be diminished—
fizzing away to nothing.
It seems unbelievable

that all of this state
is harnessed
to pains production

and prolonging. It's
as if a terribly efficient general had taken
ownership, and mounted up

baton charged every movement that resists.
For equality and freedom.
Stamping on the faces of the casualties.

here again

where the red cat with white straight legs looks out
its red ears pointed to five past the hour, and five to

here again

where the weeping woman juts forward from panes
of yellow and red, and almost loses

one eye to the shade   here again

where books line up on the shelves and where Lenin is
striding out of Shostakovich's

Symphony number 12   here again

where Jack Seabury's much worked painting
of a woman faces me, her yellow body lined, her dark

rubbed at eyes drawing me in   here again

where the peace lily forces leaves to a profusion
sprouting from a reticulated clay pot

at the exact centre of the black slate mantelpiece where . . .

imperfectness

is when the strength of light passes
and everything gathers timber
dampened down
and slickered nests burrow deep into thatch for snug

the over-grown loses colour, sags, and topples
fruit fall rots and all is sallow and jellies spongily

to mud streams threaded and waiting wild
impatient for what ebb and flow

will climb the cliffs, crumble them, and is
arrived here as Forshaw Demolition
                          the mechanical tearing
                                    back at the rind
                                              to rip

Untitled 8

an arm rises from the river
a grey-blue-pink sleeve, once, and again

drops back on itself along its own length
is withdrawn, or pulled back in

and that is how this day is
like the long returning salmon

Scan.

Is the black an atmosphere, or mud-flats, or fluid?
White body? The white
appears intact inside of the sound
                         of itself,
a heart is beating loosed
          within pale overarchings,
—a bud yearning to spring open
whatever lock restrains
so that what was a chamber of stillness
breaks to be released,
             reaches.
Is it weightless?
             Aware of its own weightlessness?
I am anxious of the unknown, for it,
its diaphragm rises and falls and rises in
'practise breaths'
the Midwife says, as she measures and listens
                         —and we all listen
to blood's flow through arteries and veins.
This is the cord in section,
                  a section through the cord.
Why then does this machine not show it
reaching out and running like a cable should
and plugging in shocking us deep beneath our skin.
This is the landscape of the nose, the open
mouth. I remember
hearing memory begins

when words are used for things.

Dust 1.

We lie bathed in faint reports
of a universe where matter spirals
to black holes, and all roads
lead to the past.

Only seeing how it was
we are drawn to the light.
Two moths tasting indifferent air
burnt by space, without a care.

The Black Eye Galaxy has a rash
of hot blue stars. The Ghost
Head Nebula's unblinking eyes
are boiling clouds. A host

of casual encounters bearing little signs
are a dark matter weaves and binds.

Dust 2.

Pheromones draw two moths
who taste the indifferent air burnt space.

Their flattened wings are mosaics
that beat of a clouded yellow dust
the soot of Black Eye Galaxies.

Their bodies shaggy cocoons will fruit
this bed with a rash of hot blue stars
that blossom and wither, and the boiling cloud

eyes of the Ghost Head Nebula earthbound
trapped beneath the skylight
are night tell stars in a happy curl

enfolding the bald moon in a scud of cloud
as matter spirals into black holes, and all
of what was, is, as every thing fails
                                            always

—

she travelled on a ticket printed from her phone
to see a robin perched on a litter bin
a man carrying a child's pink umbrella
and breakfast—english or continental

trees grow in the high gutters
rust eats at the window bars

open the windows let air disturb
the light here
let the sound of traffic bounce off
of the buildings swifts fly
to the river

it is water, she says
quenches thirst
it is the flow in blood
that bursts—
those patterned blue waves are ripped chaos

in day's early glow

he lifted the skirts of the gown of his body
to float listing
away
crossing
the decaying leaves moving towards the edge

where I left him

later that day a fox
paused red
crossing a field
having abandoned the cover of one body
of trees to make for another . . . .

the distance between us increases

the yellow day's before—

cloud like wool
with the undercoat
of lanolin
sweated out

the failure to treat
carries within it all of the shortcomings
of its own particular

an aftermath
of stretching occurs

something wild and unrestrainedly alert
is soft-padding outside of the border
waiting
                    for that step out
                                        into the open

where every possibility is—

where the sky is earthed
and floodwaters form a lake
to encircle the trees who take strange shapes in the air
like molten wax pored into cold water

In the time of Pandemic

reading the words
'the inconceivable patience
of disillusionment'

is not enough
oxygen in the night
to fuel his dreams
and thought of fundamental change
forms a cloud of dust
he daresn't strut
through wearin' times
worn thin
black crow coat

this house, the house that lived
all seasons
oriented to children
is subject to an occupation
is overrun
freedom has been taken
and it is become a retreat
a place of isolation

each thread he makes
of the days shared words and gestures
will continually break—

death, the dead, come closer

to live we follow the scientific advice
politicians hide behind
to be thought unaccountable
for all their many blunders

whatever is
below the surface shifts
clears a forest
to empty space where
imprisoned by ourselves
we exercise hearing
of those that are ill
or who died

we fear hospitals
crowded places
any contact
with other people

there is a mouth greased with consuming the World

how clean water is
now every stream refreshes—
the cork stoppered carafe
washes

is consoled, washes

there is music too sad to be borne
familiar books that can not be read—
it is necessary to breathe yourself clear of

there are dreams of losing children
parents, ourselves
thoughts repressed
rise through nights surface

enforced idleness passes, but slowly

inside the heart
a labyrinth of walls
locks, and key words
forms about her, a compass needle
whose intricacies of gold and silver
inlay are sweetened by
honey and ground almond

outside, the life that hides
comes to, the newly quiet
is shy, timid, looks about

in good time
she will take him to the grandfathers
who live where the men of the street are
wearing light suits
in the full sun
maze of the city

soon enough
they will study the pictures in Bellas Artes
drink a glass of white wine
eat from a little dish of jade olives
find that the joy hidden in a small salad
of tomato, onion, and lettuce is
a single splash of vinegar

they will be lost in the rain
of seven languages, and short arms
long ears, large hands
and small pockets

a tapestry of handmade rough
woven texture, of stolen looks
of collage books
and a silhouette tree with a knucklebone branch, where
two black birds sit side by side
patiently, patiently
will be a distraction

outside are empty beds
clothes cool for the charity shops
all of those orphaned belongings

there is an invisible killer
stalking with no purpose
except to be

we play games together
all the time apart
Skype in group chat
laugh in absentia
buy food for those who are

most vulnerable

some shrink to faces on the wall

they will lose days
slate faced waiting
for the mountains to break
for the diaphanous sky of the lake's glassy surface
to part
before their shared thought

wait, while the bales of hay from Oystercatcher fields
are an unease taken
into larder barns for the uncertain winter

wait as the keeked black and white V's fly near
for life is the luminous ghosting blue dart tremor of a kingfisher
a single pulse
passing just where the dry clay bank of the Eden gives way

is a deer leaping barbed wire

is a heron snatching fish from the river
a slither continuance for the nest

wait here—translated to fox kind, wet
-eyed snouting for the foul
transmission air
curiously sensing where
life struggling
earth cleared of all
of all of the growing years
holds

we dandelion heads are

spheres whose pale lights
are translucent pin-wheels
winked out
to feed small birds
the air pushes across where

indifferent to us, bramble are
struggling arms breaking free
to straggle in barbed leaf
bursts as if wrestling themselves
to grapple something
all snaggle stems, all tears

electricity power lines cross in series
tower to tower—mid air

a little fire, far away
gorse spines glower thickening
a sand path matter clouds

metallic glint flies fly
cow shit pats we pass by

eden becalmed
has those bottle green dappled depths that follow rain
wind turns to thin white lines
of scurry crossing

ageless it returns

even in hot it winds
sluggishly pressing
to the estuary

it too is indifferent

atwitter a
hawthorn staggers caught
in the act of stumbling, it
sputters milkweed flowers
snow cluster, spilt cream spatter
all its own

only bullocks fattening are
curious of us
coming in close
from the five barbed gate
where they sat together in a parliament
of sorts
to stand and stare at us—seriously content
silent as mourners

lonely crow

is a reminder
of good manners   or at least
of keeping the peace

days pass and cool
comes like a woman will
according to her notion

of how things are between them
as if something stowed away
is retrieved then that could be relied upon

as proof against the cold

there is a figure in the distance
in the half wild struggling
off road to climb against the drama of the skies

whose indeterminacy a veil of sorts
is thin and piercing like
the unexpected touch of a particular hand

a friendly face encountered in a strange land
or forgotten troubles wakened out of the blue
and the whole body breaks into blossom

at a time when there are no bees or butterflies
                              no pollinators of any kind
head to toe still and afraid of the silence that was the wild

what is there to find
when order has left the world and she is gone
who would sing unregulated life into every thing

what could be born(e)
when even the subterranean worm has nothing to gnaw on
is reaching stretched and thin

when every crow is another crow's brother another crow's twin
is a lookout of sorts at the furrows brim   waiting
for violence for the violence that is always there at an ending

on the 28th

the blow, sporadic, erratic, blustery
nods through the flourished whites and pinks
of marjoram and oregano
pushes bulrushes that push back
makes feverfew wave so low it almost overbalances
                festooned as it is with white and yellow
even the heavy fruit trees give and take
while inside of its bowl the pond surface calms
its many greens, browns, and silver-sky glints
the fragments of a shattered mirror
hint at what life is in the sludge-bedded deep
put an ear to it   hear it breath
whatever is sleeping there could waken
take us to where this light petters water to air

a philosophical provocation

this tree is both an assertion and a dialogue
it is ambiguous and playfully sets out in branches
it is rooting too slowly to appreciate in inches
it is not just itself but also lichens and mosses
aggregate on its surfaces, and the spine of trunk
is a book of record in a way, and the flat leaf
a translator of light and air and water, a sheathe
of cares where a slaughter of aphids turn gunk
and tear into a million chews, or that tree frogs
may choose to hide beneath and snooze, or foxes
paw at when they parachute loose, and so this
is an interpretation, and that is all it is, a miss
heard call, a faint echo, an accumulation of
words sighing like leaves on a tree, or a stove
that is ready to cook the meal that's inside it.
This door is blind shut and we don't know it's lit.

acknowledgements

'A Philosophical Provocation' was a prize winner in the Arvon International Poetry competition, and subsequently was published in *Poetry Review*.

'Ivy' was published in the Cumbrian anthology *into a gathering*.

'over the river' was published in *The Dawntreader* magazine.

'a rabbit pattered field', 'the newt', and 'wounded thunder groaned' were published in *The Journal*.

'opium poppies' was published in *Cannons Mouth* magazine.

'Catalogue for the illusory future' was published in *Speakeasy Magazine* under the title 'at the far end'.

'The air is scented by onions' was published in *Speakeasy Magazine*.

'Conjuring tree-bug' was in the anthology *Poetry for a purpose* published by Caldew Press.

'Ivy', 'Heron', 'Mayflies', 'Wasp' and 'a philosophical provocation' were also in the collection *The Lost Box of Eyes* published by The Onslaught Press in 2016.

Some of these poems were first aired at The Speakeasy, Carlisle, at Lend me your ears, at Cakes and Ale cafe, Carlisle, and at The Poetry Symposium, Carlisle, organised by Andrew Hopkins.

I would like to thank my understanding editor Mathew Staunton.
Also, I would like to thank Andy Hopkins, Marion McCready, and Becca Roberts who have been first readers of many of these poems.

Additionally, I would like to acknowledge the various teachings of St Nicholas Allotments, and the St Nicholas Allotments Association.

Alan John Stubbs has published three other
collections with The Onslaught Press

The Lost Box of Eyes (2016)
Ident (2016)
Tomorrow is the Tugboat of Today (2018)

Two of his poems can also be found in the
Onslaught anthology

to kingdom come: voices against political violence (2016)

all of these titles are available at

onslaughtpress.com

Lightning Source UK Ltd.
Milton Keynes UK
UKHW041107241120
373991UK00001B/29

9 781912 111855